The stories at this level

These stories are fuller and a littl
They introduce a greater numbe
of West Street. The words are repeated less frequently
are longer. At this level you should begin to emphasize the child's
independent reading more.

Before you start reading with your children, read the story and activities
first yourself, so that you become familiar with the text and the best way to
give it expression and emphasis when reading it aloud.

Always sit comfortably with your child, so that both of you can see the
book easily.

Read the story to your child, making it sound as interesting as possible.
Add comments on the story and the pictures if you wish. Encourage your
child to participate actively in the reading, to turn over the pages, and to
become involved in the story and characters.

This may be enough for one sitting, but don't give your child the idea that
the book is finished with. Encourage your child to take the book away and
to look through it alone.

Next time you look at the book with your child, suggest "Let's read the
story together. You join in with me." The text in the speech bubbles is often
the same as the text at the bottom of the page, so one of you can read the
text in the bubbles, and one can read the text at the bottom of the page.
This time encourage your child to guess words from the context.
Follow the words with your finger under them as you read. Don't stop
to repeat words; keep the interest up and the story line flowing along.

Now ask your child, "Do you want to read the story to me this time?"
If your child would like to do this, join in where necessary if help is needed.

The activities at this level

The activities at the back of the book need not be completed at once.
They are not a test, but will help your child to remember the words and

stories and to develop further the skills required for becoming a fluent reader.

The activities are often divided into three parts.

One part is designed to encourage you both to talk about the stories, and to link them where possible with your child's own experiences. Encourage your child to predict what will happen and to recall the main events of the story. Change the wording of the story as much as you like and encourage your children to tell you about the story in their own way.

One part encourages children to look back through the book to find general or specific things in the text or the pictures. Your child learns to begin to look at the text itself, and to recognise individual words and letters more precisely. The activities state clearly when you should give a letter its name, and when you should sound it out. The activities also introduce more writing, largely copying from words in the original story. If your children find this too difficult, copy the words onto a piece of paper for them to trace over.

One part suggests drawing or writing activities which will help your children feel they are contributing actively to the story in the book.

When you and your child have finished all the activities, read the story together again before you move on to another book. Your child should now feel secure with it and enjoy being able to read the story to you.

The little train

by Helen Arnold

Illustrated by Tony Kenyon and Sue Lisansky

A Piccolo Original
In association with Macmillan Education

Anna and Tony are playing.

Ben wants to play too.

Go away, Ben.
Come here, Ben.

The little train.

Read it please, Mama.
It's a good story.

8

The little train puffed.

Puff. Puff.

It went fast.

It came to a hill.

Puff. Puff.

The little train tried
to go up the hill.

It puffed and puffed.

The little train puffed up the hill.

Puff. Puff. Puff.

The little train did not go
so fast now.

I hope I can.
I hope I can.

19

The little train went
very slowly.

It puffed and puffed up
the hill.

The little train was near
the top of the hill.

The little train puffed down
the hill.

The little train was happy.

The little train was happy.

26

Puff. Puff.

27

Things to talk about with your children

There are two trains in this book. One was a real train, and one was a toy one.

Who was playing with the toy train?

What were both trains trying to do?

Can you find the first picture of the toy train?

Can you find the first picture of the real train?

Looking at pictures and words with your children

1. What did the train say when it began to go up the hill?
What did the train say when it was puffing up the hill?
What did the train say when it was nearly at the top of the hill?

Make three cards. Write this sentence on each card:

I ＿＿＿ I can.

Ask your child to find the right page in the story and copy the missing word onto each card for·
when the train was beginning to go up the hill (page 19)
when the train was half way up the hill (page 22)
when the train was nearly at the top of the hill (page 24)

Your child might like to draw pictures to go with each card.

2. Here is part of the story. Let's read it together. Something funny has happened to some of the words — they've been printed back to front! Can you point to the words which are written back to front? (Make sure you read the words aloud correctly.)

The little niart puffed.

Puff, ffup.

It came ot a llih.

It went tsaf.

Would you like to try writing the words the right way round?

3. The word $fast$ begins with the sound f (Point it out on page 11.)

Can you find a word in the story with two fs at the end? (puff)
Can you read it?

The word $little$ begins with the sound l (Point it out on page 9.)

Can you find a word in the story with two ls at the end? (hill)

Things for your child to do

What do you think might happen when the little train gets to the next station? Help your child to make up another story and draw pictures about the little train.

These activities and skills:	will help your children to:
Looking and remembering	hold a story in their heads, retell it in their own words.
Listening, being able to tell the difference between sounds	remember sounds in words and link spoken words with the words they see in print.
Naming things and using different words to explain or retell events	recognise different words in print, build their vocabulary and guess at the meaning of words.
Matching, seeing patterns, similarities and differences	recognise letters, see patterns within words, use the patterns to read 'new' words and split long words into syllables.
Knowing the grammatical patterns of spoken language	guess the word-order in reading.
Anticipating what is likely to happen next in a story	guess what the next sentence or event is likely to be about.
Colouring, getting control of pencils and pens, copying and spelling	produce their own writing, which will help them to understand the way English is written.
Understanding new experiences by linking them to what they already know	read with understanding and think about what they have read.
Understanding their own feelings and those of others	enjoy and respond to stories and identify with the characters.

First published 1988 by Pan Books Ltd, Cavaye Place, London SW10 9PG

9 8 7 6 5 4 3 2 1

Editorial consultant: Donna Bailey

© Pan Books Ltd and Macmillan Publishers Ltd 1988. Text © Helen Arnold 1988

British Library Cataloguing in Publication Data
Arnold, Helen
The little train. — (Read together. Level 2).
I. Title   II. Series
428.6   PE1119
ISBN 0–330–30216–7

Printed in Hong Kong